Momaya

Poetry Review 2019

MASKS

Momaya

Poetry Review 2019

MASKS

A Momaya Press Publication
London, U.K. & Wallingford, Vermont, U.S.A

All Rights Reserved
Copyright © 2019 Momaya Press and Poets
Cover, Interior Design and Layout by Maya Cointreau
Editing by Maya Cointreau & Monisha Saldanha

This book is sold subject to the condition that it shall not,
by way of trade or otherwise, be lent, resold, hired out,
or otherwise circulated without the publisher's prior
consent in any form of binding or cover other than that in
which it was published and without a similar condition
including this condition being imposed on the
subsequent publisher.

Published 2019 Momaya Press, An Earth Lodge™ Imprint.
The moral right of Momaya Press has been asserted.

ISBN 978-1-951843-02-1

TABLE OF CONTENTS

Introduction

1 The General's Widow, Mary Mulholland, First Place

2 Folded and Creased, Ash Marie Tandoc, Second Place

4 Cloud Mask, Yvonne Brewer, Third Place

5 Esar Aadil, Mind the Gap

7 Window Dressing, Maritha Amey

9 That's Society, Theodore Arthur

11 Make Up, Suzan Atasu

13 Standard Class, Aidan Baker

14 Personas - An Oresteia, James Baty

18 Not to be Defined, Shira Ben Arzi-Flom

19 Her Face, Andrew Bramwell

20 The Rock of Cashel, David Dixon

23 The Unmasking, Ruth Flanagan

25 Face Forward, James Geehring

27 Opal Eyes, Maisie Granger

29 Things I Don't Say to My Therapist, Kate Green

32 Holiday Agendas, Bruce Harris

35 Viva El Devono, Bruce Harris

38 All the World's a Stage..., Stephanie Harte

39 Hidden, Marc Hawkins

44 The Metaphorical Mask, Abbie Jones

47 In the Wilds (An Elysienne Sonnet), Ellis Logan
48 Cryptic Honesty, Joseph Marshall
51 The Shop of Masks, Fatema Matin
54 Carnival of Freedom, Zwivhuya Phoebe Mudau
56 The Chemistry of Tears, Mary Mulholland
58 Inside the Black Helmet, Orian Norfolk
60 His Mask, Brianna Ross
62 Casanova Masque, Les Thomas
64 Manikinesque, Steve Watson
65 Under My Skin, Bret White
67 Cautionary Tale, Haley White
68 The Hospital Visit, M Valentine Williams
70 About the Poets
79 About Momaya

INTRODUCTION

When you remove your MASK, the truth shines forth.

We all wear masks, shields that hide our deepest fears and emotions from the world, facades we put on at work, with family or friends. Other masks are physical, like the ones worn at kabuki theatre, to masked balls, or in the trenches of war. This year, 32 poets explore the seen and unseen within this year's theme and show us where the truth really lies.

Enjoy!
Maya & Monisha
Directors, Momaya Press

THE GENERAL'S WIDOW

Mary Mulholland

The world sees only her public face,
all pearls and smiles, but when he dies,
she locks the door, busies herself
on their once-shared bed now covered
with a pink satin spread. She's making a
cast of her husband's head. She'll paint it
bright to adorn the mantelshelf, replace
those snaps of his sons and 'himself'.

Still she can smell his cigars in the air
as she sits at noon in his fireside chair,
contemplating her scarlet masterpiece.
The funeral's over, such a release,
she'll spend the night making paper planes,
hurl them at his red eyes, nose and brains.

FOLDED AND CREASED

Ash Marie Tandoc

we are all origami children
folded into ourselves
tucking away our insides
as best as possible
to make sure the brightest selves
reflect off our shiny outsides
we are only pretty the
more you cover up

folded into ourselves,
we speak nothing
communication is a confession
uncontained in a box
no one ordained to wash them away
lines of all we wanted to say
blanketed in creases, folded and unfolded, follow the
lines already drawn

we are calm, composed
with poise and minimal disarray
we hope
that even with paper wings
we are strong enough to carry
ourselves to better places
yet, for that,
we must be crafted and shaped
by stronger hands than ours can become

that's all we can be:
folded into someone else's palms
beautified by someone else's wishes

keep us on shelves
like hollow trophies
let us collect dust
and become forgotten

CLOUD MASK

Yvonne Brewer

You pressed a feather print in the sky.
The sky did not refuse to sit back
and watch it fade.

Cloud bird, your wings paint my pain
as you fly on, never counting
unfinished lines blinded strokes made.

Feathers, clouds, leaves know
how to let go, how to fall softly, how to drift on
disappearing into new ways of being.
Something I never learned.

Dark circles, spinning rain pools
masked by sunshine smiles,
dropping tears under cloud cover
recycling toxic lies.

MIND THE GAP

Esar Aadil

I'm hosting New York's finest
and still springing trains with
strangers, faking a city-wise strength
(when I can remember how), telling
myself, "Oh! It can't possibly
rain all day."

A fucking pipsqueak, scrumpy'n
western, punk ethos'd turf sod, Salt
Lake City slurp, hand-poked all the way to
hell. But damn! Was I in love! Never
brought a sour word into the sheets,
racing to Stockholm – the dipsy

goose nabbing the Stutterheim for
insurance as you hiss steam. No, no.
It is impossible for me to outgrow and/or
abandon my roots, to become the
queen consort your working class heart

despises (yet you want me to be).

Now I'm on the fire escape, absolutely stranded,
smoking my way through the debris field of
our shared memories. Praise Be! I think
I'm getting this, learnin' to "mind the gap"

between us. On my read,
the woman he dreams of, happy
in all his weather- she is God
and he, the greatest goddamn unbeliever.

WINDOW DRESSING

Maritha Amey

My smile is always perfect
The angle always measured
The symmetry is faultless
The look sophisticated

My clothes are always structured
My nails are well-constructed
My life beautifully packaged
My children well presented

I'm always window dressing
On Facebook all impressing
At parties always raving
Yet lips are always quiv'ring

Look close beneath the surface
My eyes are always watered
Emotions always scattered
My heart is always battered

I live with constant pressure
To have a perfect stature
Guided by current fashion
To show 'AccomplisheD!' caption

I'm always window dressing
Constantly all impressing
Yet failing at succeeding
In being truly happy

THAT'S SOCIETY

Theodore Arthur

People wearing headphones
Listening to monotones
Sitting on accessibility seats
Ignoring those with a disability.
That's society.

People walking in the rain
Taking on all the strain
Their tears go nowhere but fall
Into the drain.
That's society

In the news someone gets a knife
A life cut too soon.
They fight over drugs,
When all they need is love and hugs.
That's society

People in politics talk about Brexit
Wondering how they can fix it.
Telling everyone lies
Not listening to the public's cries.
That's society.

MAKE UP

Suzan Atasu

Mother
You were always so glamorous
Back in the early years
And even when you were ill
You still made an effort
I understand because I do the same
I sit in front of the mirror
Without really looking
And I draw a line

The line I draw goes round
Round the discomfort ignores the tears
The line reminds me enough is enough
İt's time to wrap things up
..and face the world
İt's a way of drawing myself in
As well as to appear presentable
But the eyes are too wet still

Your eyes at times
Could be like looking into the end of a double barreled
    shot gun
You remember don't you?
The firing line?
And other lines worthy of mention

Bit calmer?
Yes
...calmer
Good
Now finish your face off
And go outside

STANDARD CLASS

Aidan Baker

The mask of no eye contact, when walking past a beggar,
fits most of us, I reckon, on most streets.
You wore it fixed and you were the still ones
on the train, in other passengers' booked seats.
No selling masks to you whose bad
has pulled your faces into tweets.
Too late. You took a risk against the card,
against the wheels, the racing. Now it's known. Hard.

PERSONAS - AN ORESTEIA

James Baty

Remember the baths where you were slain

I
Agamemnon

The lacquer's cracked
in tributaries,
and the gods drop madly from the eaves
like falcons' pranks.

This mask has one reality:
ridged and shrieking brows beneath the fingers,
the shape of mouth-spout lurching forth,
and it has another,
which is seen when the watchman stirs for the far-off
    fire,
when the unseen king is killed
behind these doors.

II
Libation Bearers

The hand that lifts the mask to lips
and the voice that sounds
are not the same it is this the
mother cannot see

she cannot tell that
son who lifts the knife
and son was slain
are not the same it is this the
unknown father does not see
does not tell
behind these doors

these masks have voices

III
Eumenides

Spit of rock.

Spout of rock projecting,
where goddess steps down
as if fresh-rappelled
from a chinook.

Quiet now,

watch
the magic
start.

First they are ravens,
croak-and-clawing round his head but
they lose their feathers growing fur in
patches their beaks' hard knife is
blunting to a snout.

They are jackals, then,
are dogs that growl and sniff each other
strain to catch the trail that led them all
from Argos to this rock,
where the verdict
like a witch's spell
softens them yet further.

Hush,

there's more to come.

Push the muzzle back.
Square those sharp-tipped teeth.
Round out the snapping ears.
With a firm hand straighten out the back-blown legs

and,
with two licked fingers,
pinch that wild glow inside the eyes
to leave an ember only,
curling round its tail.

They are women now.
These things that once were dogs and
birds now wear the masks of
women.

We have reached this point.
We may go no further.

IV
Proteus

The mask that once was lifted,
once was held,
now holds itself against the skin –

the varnished cracks
a thousand threads,
knot themselves to the face's lines.

As the stagehands pack away,
the mask surveys the stands.

NOT TO BE DEFINED

Shira Ben Arzi-Flom

Never bow your head.
clutch the pain tightly and release it gradually into the
facade. stay upright, always in control.

Harness the pain and you can ride into the sky. Leave
behind you a wild trail and a memorable sound of
wings. you are not to be defined. you are not to be
enclosed. You are a figure without boundaries,
wandering around a phony reality.

You could live for eternity. your piercing glance reveals
the truth behind the mask, which men try vigorously to
conceal. Create out of the pain, out of the passion, out
of the agony. Merely keep creating.

Man is nothing but a show, a performance with several
acts. until conclusion. Then the curtain lowers. But you,
you will move on in space.

HER FACE

Andrew Bramwell

Ash white is her face,
the texture of alabaster
in a folding sea.

In the lidded curls
of that instant,
her eyes like pyramids.

And sadness
moved from her lips
Into a tremor.

Her gaze in distance
bridged the time,
from there to here.

THE ROCK OF CASHEL

David Dixon

From the 'Tower of Babel' to this pilgrims cell,
I'm the penitent in the mask on the 'Rock of Cashel.'
In the sanctum of this dungeon in this cold stone jail
My mind keeps returning to the Maid of Kinsale.
Our eyes met by chance at the 'Fair of Ballymoon,'
That's a midsummer dance at the end of June,
The prettiest colleen at the county ball,
The band struck up and we danced till dawn.

We danced a gig; we reeled a reel,
stepped out a ceili and joined a square quadrille
The happiest night of my entire life,
I determined in a trice that I would make her my wife.
We would meet in secret on the 'Black Lough' shore,
Where we made an oath to be true, a troth.
Her father was the chief of the Mulligan clan
And when told I was her suitor swore "I was a dead
   man."

Waylaid on the road to our clandestine tryst,
I was clubbed and beaten in a flurry of fists.
Thrown down a shoot into a pitch black vault,
It was many days before they dragged me out.
Manacled and chained to a heavy stone,
I was sold to a Turk in a long white robe.
They rowed me to a galley, moored out in the sound,
A 'Barbary Slaver,' Morocco Bound.

Confined in the hold of this worm riddled sieve
We had to man the pumps if we wanted to live.
We bailed day and night so she did not founder,
Till we reached the sands of the 'Great Sahara.'
Whipped into a pound; by the merciless sailors,
We were sold into bondage to the Arab traders.
Tethered by the neck on a leash of chain,
We were marched across the desert in a camel train.

We walked for weeks in the blistering heat,
When my shoes fell apart; I walked on in bare feet.
The trail was marked by the bones of beast and man,
An epitaph to those who fell in the sand.
My skin turned black, we stumbled on,
Till we reached the Casbah of Dar-el-Salem.
Lashed to a pillar at the slave bazaar,
I was bought by a Jew with a jagged scar.

Transported in a cage by camel caravan,
I was brought to the 'Palace of Babylon.'

There I laboured; a beast of burden,
Pressed into service for the 'Caliph of Persia.'
Ten years passed; then it was rumoured,
That the Caliph was meeting with the 'Order of St
  Vincent,'
That's a charitable mission seeking the redemption,
Of Christian prisoners; by the paying of a ransom.

Released into the hands of this compassionate order,
We sailed for 'Valletta' on the 'Isle of Malta.'
This holy citadel of Crusader might,
This bastion of Hospitaller's, Templar's and knights,
Restored my strength to both body and mind,
And gave me passage back to the 'Shamrock Isle.'
Disguised as a monk in a mask of penance,
I went forth to wreak my plan of vengeance,

Now dressed in the cowl of a Jesuit Friar;
I entered the stronghold of the Mulligan lair,
I bade him kneel, I told him heaven,
Had sent me to hear, his last confession.
Concealed in the folds of my priestly robe,
I unsheathed the knife and slit his throat.
From the 'Tower of Babel' to this pilgrims cell,
I'm the penitent in the mask on the 'Rock of Cashel.'

THE UNMASKING

Ruth Flanagan

He ran into the grey,
the smoke engulfing him;
swallowed like a mouse in a cat's throat.
Through the belching cars,
across the road and into a narrow street.
Buildings towering above him,
leaning towards him,
drowning him in blocks of silence.

A break in the stone.
Blue skies and white cloud.
A dog barks.
A newspaper stand.
An old man sucks on a pipe
and waves the paper as he races by.

A shadow, vanishing … gone;
lost in the grey.
A car screeches.

A siren blasts.
A child cries.
The old man wipes the billboard and writes:
Young man dies on Alexandra Street.

A knock on the door.
An officer steps inside.
Hysteria!
A woman shrieks.
"I would have helped him!" she screams,
"…told him how much I loved him.
If only I'd known.
If only…"

FACE FORWARD

James Geehring

The string that holds my mask in place, just broke while I
was out
My smiling, calm persona gone, revealing fears and
doubt.
I felt that all were watching, mask in pieces at my feet
Wry smiles upon their own masks, my misfortune quite a
treat.

The seconds seemed like minutes, as some did point and
stare
With false concern upon their masks, I knew they didn't
care.
Each tiny flaw now visible, so naked and revealed
I'd never taken time to think, of all my mask concealed.

Embarrassment with guilt and shame laid out for all to
see
My words and verses scrutinized to find hypocrisy.
Without my mask to cover, now unable to deceive

I panic as their masks display the thoughts they do
   believe.

Their gazes seem like searing flames which scorches soul
   to core
I gather pieces from my mask in hopes I might restore
The smooth and shiny visage that I'd made for life's
   display
And hope no one will notice cracks, as next act starts to
   play.

OPAL EYES

Maisie Granger

Before,
bare my chin, my cheeks, my smile
admired the lying world, unknowing its truth
as a masquerade sea.

I saw her face, a shapely design.
Floating in the plated ore of her cheekbones, her
　　shimmering gold, winked a pair of diamond encrusted
　　sapphire eyes. I was sure they shed pearls if sorrow
　　seized her.
Adoringly jealous, my fingers came feeling for precious
　　jewels of my own, only to find disappointing, ugly flesh
　　–
should my eyes shed pearls?

Back home I did not like what I could see.
With each prod of my finger, the mirror exposed
　　mediocracy.
I endeavoured to become a better me.

Daily I fell for her face, and in sympathetic likeness
I forged my own face of patches of humble tin and
    copper, latched the jigsaw to my own complexion,
    plastered a second skin.
I popped duo opals into my sockets.
I resembled her.
After that, she liked the pearls I cried.

My conscience hinted I should take it off one day,
that, one day, smoke and mirrors would end.
Yes, one day, I promised my conscience. One day.
But she liked my furnished opal eyes,
my misty gemstone tinge.

Yet my second skin was heavy to bear. One night, I tried
    to peel them off, the pieces. Just for a moment.
Poured stinging sulphur to exfoliate.
Scooped my sockets out with a spoon.
All the while, the pearls poured out.
Pop.
Opal eyes no more.

Bloodshot veins spiked my throbbing eyeballs.
This was no ruby red.
Flesh stared back at me, begging for breath.
Real tears shed.

I must restore the opals, suffocate the loud, imperfect
    flesh.

The mask was my face now.
I looked down at the opals in my open palms.
How could I put them back? I cannot un-see.
I realise my face is a mask, a phoney fake, a lie
and the beauty was all constructed to lie.

That must mean her face was a lie.

But I loved the lie, and so I married her, or she married
    me,
and in photos, I can still see my bloodshot eyes staring
    out at me.

I am ashamed, for it is the mask I loved, not she, though I
    thought it was she at the start.
It is too late.
I cannot remove my mask now, it won't come off, for
she loved my mask and not me.

Nowadays she and I, never we, wander the masquerade
    sea
side by side, stiff, permanently, fixedly smiling.
Sometimes I look at Her mask and wonder why she loves
    my mask
because I don't love hers anymore. I see her deception.

A face may love a mask
but no mask loves another.

THINGS I DON'T SAY TO MY THERAPIST

Kate Green

Some of it is a lie—but
not how you think, see—
I wear your expectations like
a blanket, the one you
tell me I can wear to feel
safe, but I
use it now to make you see—
not Me, but who you think Me is
But truth is, neither of us know who
Me is, see?

I use your breathing
exercises like a permission slip, a
hall pass to panic in the grocery
store, where few can tell the difference
between organic trauma and imitation—
But even here in your office, between trying to
seek out the seeds of truth from the
weeds of memory, I throw wide

the doors to my closet of lies and
choose which mask to wear today.

HOLIDAY AGENDAS

Bruce Harris

The driver has separate names, roles and beings,
according to pants, circumstance and situation.
Ben Foster is the neighbour, employee, voter,
Uncle Ben, Ben and Dad are all the family men,
Benny F. and Foster B. the pub and the payslip.
He secretly wishes his Ford Focus was a Porsche
and worries about petrol, its prices and effects.

'I'm trying to do them all the best that I know how
but I still need inspiration, the wit to improvise,
somewhere on the Dad range between tyrant and clown
and if not Solomon, away from gormless geek'.

Front seat passenger still remembers Planet Girl
when all and nothing simultaneously mattered
and the name list was Jennifer, Jenny cute and Jen for
   friends,
and didn't include Mum or Mrs. Someone else.

She has occasional guilty day dreams in a guise of femme
  fatale
and even if wealth is evil, she'd still like to have a go.

'It's Janus masks, juggling acts, white lies, negotiations,
the pendulum from shrew to saint hovering in between.
I don't always do the words, but I'm not bad at the roles
and if no domestic goddess, I can do the hanging in
  there'.

Back seat right is still stalking Planet Teen
and words are often 'like', 'whatever', 'so' and 'what?'
She's now on her phone and then on social media,
checking out Sally's crowd, who's news, who's history.
She wishes for less blankness on the canvas of her future
and doesn't trust the notion of love for ever after.

'Some days it's like a spotlight has selected me to follow
and other days I lurch about, stumbling through a jungle.
I'm afraid of desert islands and the challenges of alone,
and falling so far short of star that I can only be a
  shadow'.

Back seat left is baby James, a child when childhood
  suits,
with a small sporadic man sometimes growling in the
  guts.
Babies usually get their way, but James already knows
that head pats and goo-goo talk are a heavy price to pay.

He is scoring, he is leading, he can hear the ceaseless
    cheering,
but he wakes in the small hours and watches darkened
    corners.

'I'm a striker, not a midfield man; I'm soldier, not civilian;
they might be older and know more, but only I know me.
I'm afraid they'll make strange shapes of me, like an
    animal balloon
and when what has to happen happens, what's left will
    not be me'.

The city streets have given way to a dominance of green;
their normal life is well rear now, and the holiday's ahead.
No refuges of work and school, no strategic masks or
    costumes,
and all that's now left facing them is a six-foot question
    mark.
Through the mornings, the afternoons and even all the
    nights,
here comes the family hive with nowhere left to hide.

'If this just proves too hard to do, escape routes are
    ahead
with more signposts and maps and less novelties and
    guesswork,
but falling at the start means the finish is a distant dot;
if we can't do eternal bonds, let us all at least be friends'.

VIVA EL DEVONO

Bruce Harris

What we see in seaside towns can never be for ever;
childhoods and old age cannot always hold together.
The ice creams, the fish and chips, the rock and candy
    floss
will be missed all the more when we realise their loss.
The most deceptive mask is now, as if now will always be,
but there could be other fates for 2090 by the sea.

Climate change has now heated up all of southern Spain
and simple daily living there is something of a pain.
Tourist hordes head off on desperate searching tours
to find better holidays on cooler, temperate shores.
And all in due course, perhaps investigation reaches
the blue skies and sweeping sands of Devon's golden
    beaches.

Two successful seasons put thousands in the know
that this part of Inglaterra esta muy fantastico;
and soon, the tourists talk to local mortgage lenders

and all along the Torquay front, they're building
   haciendas.
The people remain dubious, being generally the sorts
who always reckoned finkas were people lost in
   thoughts.

There's tapas cafes in Sidmouth, and all the catering
   sellers
are phasing out the fish and chips and starting on paellas.
During afternoons in Brixham, the people take a rest as
their former forty winks have now become siestas
and the locals really feel it's a presumptuous liberty
to build a new bull-fighting ring in Budleigh by the sea.

The English say the annoying thing, the aspect that's so
   wrong
is the failure of the tourists to learn the local tongue;
the waiters would prefer to serve chips and not patatas
and just occasionally say hello instead of 'buenos dias',
but they've come to realise they'll not sell a single cola
unless accompanied by a smile and a loud and cheery
   'hola'

The tourists argue simply that what they really like the
   most
is sitting in the sun for hours without becoming toast.
Exmouth Market now, they say, just try a day trip there;
you could be on Valencia beach, except with cooler air.

The English may not like it, but that's the way it goes;
los bandidos ingleses are fond enough of euros!

And very soon we'll integrate; no-one will think the less
of a family moving in next door called Gomez or Cortes.
Imitation Gaudis will decorate Plymouth squares
and Picasso floats appear on the annual local fairs.
The visitors will multiply, each year more and more;
so much nicer now, they'll say, than anything before.

ALL THE WORLD'S A STAGE...

Stephanie Harte

Forcing a smile
To distract from vacant eyes
Repetitive chimes
'I'm fine'
Hard gasp in
Deep breath out
Shrinking inside
Blacking out
Liquid confidence
Laughter loud
Fuel for my camouflage

'All the world's a stage...'
and I'm hidden behind what I'm playing.

HIDDEN

Marc Hawkins

You don't know me because you cannot see me.
I am staring at you eye to eye
still, you don't see me.

You live on my road, on the opposite side.
You talk with my wife
but you wouldn't recognise me if my life
depended on it.
If you did would you ask yourself why
I use this disguise?
Or why I build this façade, all synthetised
and collaged with harlequin and rags
and makeup, thick and chalk dry?

- Do you think she remembers me,
or mentions me to my kids? -

If you were to realise who I am
would you guess why I left town the way I did?

Would you question my morals?
Would you class me as a coward?
Blatantly and outwardly abandoning them,
ducking out without so much
as a clue on a post-it note,
selfishly putting the blame in their hands,
the pain in their hearts.
Would you understand if I were to tell you
that I wasn't running away from them,
I was running away from me…

- Why are they not here tonight?
I could have looked at them and
still remained invisible -

… or that the love I felt could have burst my chest
but the fear of losing that love
could have crushed my heart to pulp,
and it nearly did.
They were my light.
I tried to be theirs but couldn't
shine as brightly.

Would you explain to them, if I asked it of you,
that the breakdown wasn't their fault;
it was just another cable becoming detached,
a further break in the circuitry.
Then, even I didn't know who I was.

I convinced myself I wasn't anything
and in doing so became nothing.

-Is she with someone new?
Are they a happy family?

Would you remember that time
when you sensed our vulnerability?
When those cracks and fissures became visible.
Open to attack. Free to make your move.
Her wings broken so she couldn't rise above
and me sinking ever deeper in the mud.
You, offering a hand of friendship,
then the lips of betrayal.

- I close my eyes. It's not you
I want to see her with -

Would you face me and straight away
remember how she felt;
her satin skin, her natural scent?
Would you run through your mind every action,
tracing every step of your seduction?
Do you remember the colour of our bedroom walls,
hers and mine?
Those walls became tainted that day,
streaked with lines as black as my blood…

I forgave her straight away
but the light faded behind a veil,
and I faded with it -

Did you recognise my turmoil
or understand I was teetering on a precipice?
Hands grasping, finding nothing,
trying my hardest to air swim towards them,
my dry island.

- Does she know I was making my
way back?

You saw me and instead of throwing me
the end of a rope you pushed
and I fell
and I sank… and I ran.
Do you ever feel like a murderer feels?

- Maybe they'll…
Does she know that I died then?
Would she ever accept this me?

And there you are, with your family,
sitting and staring and laughing at me.
And me, in this ring, five feet away,
staring back from behind this mask,
juggling flaming torches for your amusement,
putting a smile on your kids faces

and you have no fucking clue who I am.
Nobody does, and that is why I am here,
because you are there
and I can take anything I want from you,
anything at all because these are my terms,
this is my stage and I am in control.
You will laugh when I make you laugh
and you will feel sad when I make you sad.
I will take your marriage with a click of my finger
and a careless word.
I will take your life and shake it
until it becomes unrecognisable
and then see where you seek your salvation.
I will kick down the folly and smash the façade.
I am the all powerful.
I see you but you don't see me.
I am hidden, I ask for nothing and I need no one.

- Tomorrow is our last night in this town.
Do you think they'll come?

THE METAPHORICAL MASK

Abbie Jones

I wear my mask to hide my fears,
To conceal the pain and falling tears.
The world will think I'm okay, I'm fine,
In reality I'm hurting, all the time.

The pain goes on and on and on,
The girl I was; she's left, she's gone.
The mask I wear is who I'll be,
Until I'm alone and it's just me.

Then I remove the mask and find,
There's barely anything left behind.
I'm broken and I'm dead inside,
I wear my mask so I can hide.

Then I don't have to try and explain,
They'll want a reason for all the pain.
But there isn't one, it's just always there,
Sometimes it's too much to bear.

I'm filled with feelings, the sadness is plenty,
Yet somehow still; I feel so empty.
I wear my mask, that holds a smile,
But it can only last a while.

The girl they see is happy and shy,
They do not know it's all a lie.
I'm dying to let the real me out,
She's trapped inside, can't you hear her shout?

I'm not really shy, not quiet at all,
But my mask is so big, it makes me feel small.
It covers so much, there's lots to hide,
I have to keep it all inside.

My mask is good, I wear it well,
It shows the story I want to tell.
Of a girl who's happy, she's care-free,
How I wish that was actually me.

I've had enough, I can't pretend,
The mask must come off, this must end.
I step outside, ready to reveal,
The mask is off and I let myself feel.

Finally, now, at last I'm free,
This is the truth, this is me.
No more mask, the show is done,
But something's only just begun.

The scene around me starts to change,
Faces are different, something's strange.
Suddenly masks, they start to fall,
They weren't real, after all.

And just like that, they're all set free,
Slaves no more to vulnerability.
We talk and share, they feel the same,
I realise now I'm not to blame.

Sometimes we all wear masks you see,
So much to hide and pretend to be.
But when you're ready, let them fall,
You'll see you're not alone at all.

Without our mask to hide behind,
The more we realise, people are kind.
They want to help, they understand,
If you let them lend a hand.

You'll finally see, it's not just you,
There are others facing demons too.
Behind their masks, they hide as well,
Mask or not? It's hard to tell.

IN THE WILDS...AN ELYSIENNE SONNET

Ellis Logan

i walk for miles in wilds empty and still
stumble over rocks, suckle rivers sweet
feet calloused, muscles strong, and heart yet ill

love wanders not, pushes instead, insists
i must go where hearts are closeted, masked

love! don't you wonder what treasure is lost?
this lie buried is the hardest to find
a shining stone sleeps blanketed with moss

blankets, sodden and steaming, i throw off
in the night, moaning, missing, i sleep rough

waking, finding not love but stars to guide
through wilds tamed, each step brings understanding
the treasure is i and nothing gold hides

in missing you i have found myself, true

CRYPTIC HONESTY

Joseph Marshall

There's a clear sky on the coast
For there certainty ends its span
The thoughts that stay in my head
Are as clear and as set
As every hill and valley on land

But when the thoughts become words
They swim blindly into the blue
They pass from land into sea
Where they are lost in the deep
And I fear what they could mean for you

My words are like a fine quilt
Laced with truth and fabrication
With combined materials
They make for a more real
And deceptive impersonation

Cryptic honesty
Words I cannot speak
Just on the tip of my tongue
Right at the back of my throat
Teetering on the edge
Unwilling to be said

Maybe I'm deceiving us all
So I can spare myself
When you ask if I am alright
And I say that I'm fine
It's a lie
But not in the way you'd expect

It's so clear to me
And so obvious to see
Because I told it so blatantly
But no one else can see it
So how can I admit it
Other than honestly?

Cryptic honesty
Words I dare not speak
My voice restrained and hamstrung
Thoughts unable to be known
Teetering on the edge
Unwilling to be said

Maybe I'm confusing it all

So I don't have to tell
The difference between real and fake
To me it's all the same
It's no game
It's how I can live with myself

It's so clear to me
And so transparent to see
Because I told it so openly
But no one else can see it
So how can I profess it
Other than cryptically?

THE SHOP OF MASKS

Fatema Matin

Welcome to The Shop of Masks! How can I help today?
We have masks for all occasions! Let me show you sir!
  This way!

We have masks that say, "I'm fine," when someone asks
  if you're okay,
And you can't tell them the truth, about the sorrows of
  your day.

We've got masks with painted smiles, when you're
  holding back the tears,
And masks of hope, when you have none, to conceal
  your deepest fears.

We have facades of confidence, when insecurities attack.
We have sizes to fit everyone, in our stockroom at the
  back!

We also have masks of anger, to hide what's troubling
  you,
But if it's anger you want to hide, we've got masks for
  that too!

Our masks of congratulations are on offer, three for two.
For when a tide a jealousy, is washing over you.

And masks of strength are on sale, for when you can't
  break down,
When you can't show any weakness. The best bargains in
  town!

A mask of sociability is perfect when you're shy,
Or a mask of humble modesty, to help control your pride.

When you're feeling very frightened, a mask of courage
  you should use,
And use a mask of humour, to lighten any mood!

When you're anxious or you're worried, a mask of calm
  will see you through,
You'll find them over there sir, in aisle twenty-two.

The best-selling masks are those that laugh to cover pain,
And those with lots of make up, for those who are too
  vain.

Please follow user directions. Don't wear a mask for long!
Talk to those who care for you and tell them what is
wrong.

Then a mask is no longer needed, and when it's done its
task,
We happily accept refunds, here at The Shop of Masks!

CARNIVAL OF FREEDOM

Zwivhuya Phoebe Mudau

I go to Venice during the day,
and back to you when the sun sets.
I don't mean to own double residence,
but where else would I go when you have lost your
   penitence.

In Venice I find freedom, to be whoever I want to be,
before I'm back to being whatever you want me to be.

Like a mask of many colors and shapes,
I amble gracefully through the narrow streets changing
   hosts.
You sit on the panel trying to memorize me,
and in anything I say you run to plagiarize me.

Just because you know me at 8am,
doesn't mean that you know me enough for 3pm.

I'm human, I change,
I adapt, I age,
but you only choose to want to see the real me.
As if happiness is not real to me,

So,
Allow me to go to the carnival of masks during noon.
I will be back at yours, quite soon.

THE CHEMISTRY OF TEARS

Mary Mulholland

My therapist says crying is good for you.
I know people who cry.
I come from a family where tears were taboo,
a family of girls who never cried.

My dentist asks what's going on
clenching my jaws has cracked all my teeth.
But I haven't, I don't, I didn't
not when my parents died or

I got divorced or my children left home,
the kitchen flooded, the roof caved in.
I only clench slightly at Christmas.
He says I wouldn't know, it happens at night.

Nor do I sleep. Horses are put down
when they grind away their teeth.
Holding tools mid-air, he gently says,
sometimes violin strings snap.

I ask my therapist if I'm a violin.
She says, what kind of music do you play?
and like a rush I feel them, deep inside –
but that's where they stay.

INSIDE THE BLACK HELMET

Orian Norfolk

Let me measure your face, to ensure a good fit –
we have four sizes, you'll be surprised. You are a two.
Your safety is important to us, you know.
This polycarbonate visor will enable a clear view
of shrieking faces and fleeing white-soled trainers;
the triple filters, mouthparts of an alien insect,
protect you from unknown noxious liquids and fumes.
Now you are like your brothers, a dreadful wall of black,
shields and batons raised to engage the enemy.

They will see nothing of you. I admit your main purpose
is to intimidate, to terrify the unprotected, the ill-
   equipped.
Your face is hidden, they cannot tell if you are jeering
or weeping, inside this black helmet.
You know them though; their bodies, exposed and
   fragile,
are easily crushed. But they return each day.

I wonder if they know who they are fighting?
You're ready now, off you go to take your place.

HIS MASK

Brianna Ross

He looks in the mirror,
Only to see the person he is pretending to be,
He smiles and it makes him sad that smile looks so real,
That nobody has noticed it is a fake yet
It takes every part of him not to let what he is really
   feeling show

He prepares today's mask
Today he will be playing the role of the charismatic A+
   student,
He will be friendly and laugh at everyone's jokes,
Maybe even make a few of his own.

Tomorrow he will talk with his friends,
Hoping that perhaps one of them will see through his
   mask,
But knowing that he is too good of an actor for his own
   good

Maybe in a week or two he will be able to switch masks,
Seem even happier than before,
Cover his tracks before someone sees them

He wants to take off his mask,
He really does
But is afraid that if he does,
He himself will shatter

So he waits...
He wants someone to see through the mask,
But he continues to work hard to keep everything
   hidden,
Why must he do this to himself?

He is not the only one,
There are more that put on a brave face,
And hide their true feelings behind a mask
Sometimes it slowly chips away or is too thin and people
   can see right through

He is hurting,
He is struggling,
He is broken,
He is shattered,
He wears his mask

CASANOVA MASQUE

Les Thomas

My soul hovers in Venice tonight,
Dreams tangled with canal moonlight;
Signorinas at a painted masque

Invoke an ancient libertine
Some potion to scatter on the scene:
From death the mage rises, to his task.

The incantation is intense,
The air heavy with musky scents,
The dead and the living are one.

Each bridge becomes a rendezvous
For secret lovers, false or true,
And soon strange revels are begun.

Fluted columns blue visions evoke,
Moody as misty incense smoke;
Venice in its medieval trance

Through an Adriatic ballroom
Floats like a conquering bridegroom,
Who with the past must ever dance.

And all along the Rialto
The passionate idols sway and flow
In a mad marionette burlesque.

The Grand Canal's a carnival sight
To court a sated satyr of night—
A romance insanely grotesque.

And still my soul in Venice hovers
Among the veiled beguiling lovers :
Immortal shines each signorina

In her gondola of mystery,
Gliding with seductive history.
To the masque crawls Casanova.

MANIKINESQUE

Steve Watson

You look over and see me looking at you
And you try to guess what I'm feeling
And even if feeling is what I can do
I'm manikinesquely concealing.
Yes, I'm not a great one for excitement
You say I'm an inscrutable fool
And yes it's perhaps an indictment
That my good friends have numbered so few.

But still waters run deep you know
And in that sense I'm rather profound
In my verse I'm sure you'll find echoes
Of your Hardys, Eliots and Pounds.
My poetry issues from underground wells
It won't be long now before some of it sells.

UNDER MY SKIN

Bret White

What plays beneath the surface?
A placid ocean in the night,
With currents swirling underneath.
My face shows its expressions,
Like flowers bloom in Spring,
Like trees dressed for Autumn,
Yet, hiding truth beneath.

Look closer to see the scene,
Painted like a picture,
With images unseen.
What does it all mean?

The thoughts I have that swirl inside,
The thoughts I take the care to hide,
Are all placed behind the wall of Plastic,
Buried under my Skin,
Bearing a mask with emotions within.

CAUTIONARY TALE

Haley White

i do not recognize her: the round-cheeked, round-bellied
zombie with the sad eyes who catches
my gaze in medicine cabinets, mirrors, and
store front windows these days. she is run-ragged,
thick-jowled, furrow-browed, angry. she carries a
grief backpack loaded with wet rocks. the extra weight
causes poor posture and a misaligned hip. makes her say
things like, "Ohhh, my hip flexors!" when she
rises, slowly in the morning, like molasses, out of bed.
she dresses like a hostess might the day after
guests leave: bleach-stained shirt, cut-off sweats,
leftovers dried with abandon where she has
wiped her hands on her thigh rather than
walk the seven unfathomable steps required to
fetch a napkin. she is old, which is not to be
confused with elderly. old, as in no longer young.
old, as in the age you are when you start
receiving more invitations to funerals than weddings.
eye cream old.

she swears off aperitifs and nightcaps, chases
an increasingly large menagerie of morning
vitamins with tap water, considers gym memberships
    during
bouts of insomnia, wears guilt like a carefully selected
wardrobe piece she spent too much money on and
    therefore cannot stand
to see get dirty or wrinkled or stained.
She is the before picture in a self-improvement
    advertisement,
a blue-collar worker after a long double shift,
the woman in the old folks' home who has no visitors but
still turns away neighbors and nurses, all the while
refusing to get a cat. she is a cautionary tale in grief.
i do not recognize her.

THE HOSPITAL VISIT

M Valentine Williams

Masked clowns and executioners both wear
the badges of their roles, and share
the terror and the joy of being there.

When she sees me, she smiles, showing no trace of fear,
until I leave and see her wipe away a tear.
The nurse will bring her tablets on a tray,
which will not make her well, only delay
her passing from us by a single day.

The doctor, inscrutable, looks on.
Does not know what to say. His work is done.

The clown's mask is the harder one to wear.
We smile and smile; won't lay our feeling bare.
She understands this, knows how much we care.
Levity is exhausting to maintain.
She knows this, feels it, wants to ease our pain.
Our masks have slipped; we are ourselves again.

ABOUT THE POETS

Esar Awal Aadil, a Pakistani American, is beginning to understand her rich, culturally complex upbringing through poetry and travel. She practices writing as a form of self-documentation, frequently addressing issues of family dynamics, escapism, the idea of homecoming, and the trauma of putting words to paper. Esar lives in NYC working as a freelance photographer.

Maritha Amey wants to tell honest stories capturing the fears and joys of living. Stories that celebrate life with all its challenges and triumphs, of heartbreak and healing. She likes to take all of life's filters and delve into how they shape our lives. She is currently pursuing her passion of writing, coaching and promoting the cause to improve mental health and self-management for professionals.

Theodore Arthur enjoys reading fictional stories and poetry.

Suzan Atasu writes emotive personal poems. A few years ago she was writing short intimate pieces which often hinted at the sublime. Her style has developed and her latest content reflects a confidence in developing a new narrative performance style that is bold and connective. Audiences often describe her work as genuinely real and powerful, connecting with the deep emotional interplays embedded in her work.

Aidan Baker works as a librarian in Cambridge. His poems have appeared in print outlets such as Orbis, online projects organised by the writers' group 26 Characters, and other places. He blogs his published work at https://blurtmetry.blogspot.com .

James Baty recently graduated from university, where he studied French and Portuguese. He has been writing for last four years and has many of influences, particularly the modern Greek poets, such as Seferis, Cavafy, Elytis etc, as well as Alice Oswald.

Shira Ben Arzi-Flom is a poet, an advocate and a blogger. In 2016, Shira published Fly, a book meant to inspire the reader by revealing how, when faced with the impossible, the best is brought out of both famous and completely unknown individuals and as a result they are able to influence the world and make it a better place. FLY consists 49 characters taken from throughout our documented history, each one beautifully sketched and described by both the historical facts and inspirational text that sheds a unique poetic light on the subjects.

Andrew Bramwell lives in the West Midlands, England. He has been writing all of his life and has published a novel 'Karelia'. He is currently studying as a mature student at the University of Cambridge.

Yvonne Brewer lives in Cork, Ireland and has had poetry published since 2014. Her first poetry book released in October 2018. "Twigs" is a collection of poems based on the simple but extra ordinary mindful moments of everyday life combining motherhood with nature and reflecting spiritual themes that take the reader on a journey to the soul.

David Dixon for many years made his living as a shellfish diver, diving for crayfish off the North Coast of Cornwall and later diving for scallops off the West Coast of Scotland. He has also spent time salvaging shipwrecks off Cornwall and Northern France and had bouts of employment in the North Sea, and then (based in Singapore,) he spent six years in South East Asia, diving for various diving company's connected to the oil industry. In 2010 he retired, and since he's always been a big reader, (and now had plenty of time on his hands) he decided to enroll in a creative writing course which introduced him to poetry.

Ruth Flanagan is a secondary school teacher and published poet.

James Geehring lives in the U.S. and is fascinated by life. *"I am an observational poet, the world provides so many facets and details to take notice of."*

Maisie Granger is an English Literature and Creative Writing student, interested in all things unnerving.

Kate Green has been pursuing a bachelor's degree in English (with an emphasis in writing) since 2016. She has won both the President's Writing Contest Award and the Fine Arts Showcase Award (1st and 3rd place, respectively) at San Diego Christian College for her works in fiction. Additionally, she regularly volunteers as a copy editor for The Wild Rose Press.

Bruce Harris is a Devon-based author and poet who has been extensively published in both print and online magazines and consistently successful in short fiction and poetry competitions since 2004. Bruce has published three poetry anthologies: Raised Voices, Kaleidoscope, and The Huntington Hydra. Howell Grange is his first novel and he has published four collections of short fiction: First Flame, Odds Against, The Guy Thing, and A Collection of Words.

Stephanie Harte is a poet and gin distiller from Bristol. She originally trained and performed as an actress in London before finding her rightful place hidden behind the gin stills and her writing.

Marc Hawkins is a writer and a contemporary artist. Originally from Birmingham, UK, he moved to Cornwall in 2005 where he still resides.

Abbie Jones is currently studying at university and always spends her free time writing. She has been writing poetry and short stories for ten years. She has always loved the escape writing brings from day-to-day life.

Ellis Logan lives a quiet life in New England where she writes science fiction and fantasy books for all ages. Though she obsesses daily over super powers and the gods of old, she has a special place in her heart for haiku, renga, and sonnets. She is currently working on two new books, Discovery and Cursed Night, and has four published series: Inner Origins, Starseeds, Full Disclosure, and Post Magic.

Joseph Marshall is a 23 year old aspiring writer from West Wales. When he's not trying to get his novella published, he's posting poetry on his new blog, https://inkfingersentries.home.blog/ and hoping to have more of his work published in the future.

Fatema Matin won third prize in the sixth International Muslim Writers' competition in 2006 but since then has been writing at home. *"When I read the theme 'masks', I thought about the variety of situations in which we don't show how we truly feel. It was more intuitive, in some ways, to reflect upon the theme quite seriously but I tried to approach the theme with lightness and humour."*

Zwivhuya Phoebe Mudau is a 19 year old girl, born and raised in South Africa who loves to write and speak. A first-time writer, she is hoping to become a poet because Poetry is life.

Mary Mulholland turned to poetry after careers in journalism and psychotherapy. She has recently completed a Masters in Poetry from Newcastle/ The Poetry School, London, and will graduate in December. She lives in London, UK. She knows you should always turn away before putting on a mask.

Orian Norfolk is a mathematician at heart and says, *"Poetry empowers me to describe thoughts and experiences in an elegant and efficient way."*

Brianna Ross is a 14 year old amateur author, who has been writing since preschool. She often spends hours every month helping her classmates and friends edit their own stories and poetry. Although she just graduated 8th grade she had the opportunity to read a poem in a middle school Poetry Slam in 7th grade. She is working towards a career as an author and hopes to have published works before she graduates high school.

Ash Marie Tandoc is a non-binary, bisexual, Filipino-American whose works are influenced by the intersectionality of their identity, as well as by the world around them, begging to be noticed and put on paper. Ash Marie Tandoc has been published in American High School Poets Just Poetry!!! the National Poetry Quarterly, as well as in a local publication entitled the Inlandia: A Literary Journey. Tandoc hopes to expand their writing capabilities and learn how to improve.

Les Thomas was born and lives in Southsea, Hampshire, England UK. A retired Marine Safety Officer, has had verse published in the USA, stories and plays broadcast at home and in New Zealand, where he won a national award. He is writing an ambitious novel.

Steve Watson is a part-time poet.

Bret White was born in Tennessee, United States. He wrote poetry mostly to woo girls in his childhood, but it became a form to express his emotions in his teenage years. Says Bret, *"I am no master, but I enjoy the art."*

Haley White is an interdisciplinary storyteller who primarily works as a filmmaker, theatre practitioner, and arts producer. Although she has been writing poetry her entire life, she's mostly kept it to herself until now.

M Valentine Williams is a novelist and poet hiding out in Shropshire, UK. From a background in teaching and mental health but now retired, she notes the oddities of her world and tries to present them in her writing. Winner of the Hippocrates Poetry prize a while back, she reads at Welcome Trust events and helps run the writers' group she founded in her home town.

ABOUT MOMAYA

Maya Cointreau has over two decades of experience in publishing. She has written and published more than twenty books spanning the fiction, children's and non-fiction books genres. She was managing editor of *DCC Magazine* with a circulation of more than 60,000 readers and  is Director at Earth Lodge™, a publisher of literature and non-fiction books for all ages.

 **Monisha Saldanha** earned her MBA at Harvard Business School in 2001 and has been working in publishing and internet commerce ever since. She is proud that Momaya Press is increasingly recognized as the premiere worldwide forum for short stories and poetry.

HOW CAN YOU BECOME
AN AWARD-WINNING AUTHOR?

There's really just one secret – tell an amazing
story and tell it well!

Submit your short stories and poems to
momayapress.com

Printed in Poland
by Amazon Fulfillment
Poland Sp. z o.o., Wrocław

51290703R00054